Dinosaurs Are Dynamite

Another adventure in the Alpha-Bitz™ Series

(Parents, you'll be happy to know this introduces over 50 new words for your children's growing minds!)

by

Joseph Fischer

AF480319

Ankylosaurus are Aggressive

Brachiosaurus are Barbaric

Chungkingosaurus are Calculating

Dilophosaurus are Dangerous

Einiosaurus are Eerie

Fukuiraptor are Ferocious

Gastonia are Gigantic

Hesperosaurus are Hulking

Irritators are Immense

Jaxartosaurus are Jarring

Kritosaurus are Knobby

Lambeosaurus are Large

Microraptor are Mean

Nedoceratops are Nefarious

Ouranosaurus are Obtrusive

Pterodactyl are Perilous

Quaesitosaurus are Quick-Witted

Rinchenia are Rowdy

Stegosaurus are Strong

Tyrannosaurus Rex are Tough

Ugrosaurus are Unwieldy

Velociraptors are Voracious

Wendiceratops are Wild

Xenoceratops are eXtremely terrifying

Yingshanosaurus are Yelping

Zuniceratops are Zoic

Draw and Name your favorite dinosaur below

(Draw it here)

www.ingramcontent.com/pod-product-compliance
Lightning Source LLC
Chambersburg PA
CBHW042015110726
48006CB00004B/1100